Over 21 And Still Into Noddy

Over 21 And Still Into Noddy

First published May 1991 by **"A Twist in the Tale"**,
18 Hind Street, Retford, Notts, DN22 7EN

ISBN 1 87426 85 5

Printed by **PRINT iT (Nottm) Ltd**
Telephone (0602) 442063 - ask for Ian

Typeset by **Chris and Candy Chuter**
Telephone (0332) 662032

Cover design by **Martin Cookson and Paul Cookson**

Cover photograph by **J.L.Harrop**

Thanks to:
Sally, Martin, Noddy, Colin Newman, Malcolm, Nomis, Trev and everyone at the Slade International Fan Club.

Slade International Fan Club, PO Box 4YD, London W1A 4YD

Dedicated to Sally

Introduction by Noddy Holder

Paul's poems cover the whole spectrum of everyone's emotions - the innocence of childhood memories, the fantasies of adolescence, the fight for good over evil and of course the never ending rigours of love.

His sharp observations and clever use of the written word make the pages come alive and help to conjure up the feeling that you're listening to an old and trusted friend pouring out his innermost thoughts.

How someone who grew up on a diet of Slade and Batman came out of it unscathed and with his brain still in good working order is beyond belief. (Paul did and has.)

Read on and I guarantee that you won't be disappointed . . .

Keep On Rockin'

Noddy Holder

This collection brings together selected poems from already published and now deleted collections together with a substantial body of new work.

Selection was never an easy task and ultimately some pieces have been excluded although these may still see the light of day in a more performance based collection.

Although tempted to rewrite and restructure earlier pieces I have kept this to a minimum and wherever possible the poems have been placed in a broad chronological order throughout.

Well, here you have it then ... Paul Cookson's Selected Poems 1979 - 1991, over ten years of my life and (well) over 21 and still into Noddy ...

Paul Cookson

Some of these poems have appeared in the following publications:

You Took The Words Out Of My Mouth	1980
A Twist In The Tale	1981, 1982, 1984
Waiting For The ZAP!	1984
More Than A Badge	1986
Unclench The Fists	1989
Sketches	1989

Contents

1979 - 1989

Batman May Have Saved the World but He Never Wrote Good Poetry

Looking back on childhood
I remember how, with youthful vision
I wanted to cast off my infant uniform
of duffle coat and short grey trousers
and attire myself in the essential blue tights, red y fronts and cape
so that I may be recognised as a hero,
saving the human race my everyday occupation.

But, looking back,
the blue tights were wrinkled, the cape too big and the y fronts baggy.
I never acquired x-ray vision or the taste for spinach.
Instead, I only fastened my duffle coat at the neck,
swung tiny fist in a slow-motioned K - E - R - P - O - W !
and painted myself green a couple of times
until I had grown anonymously out of short trousers.
No front page revelations of daring escapades.
No earth shattering stories of the saving of humankind
with only two seconds and a laser-proof medallion to spare
or deadly mortal combat with nasty villains whose goal is
world domination with the aid of android vampire hamsters.
No last minute miracles and getaways due to the lack of
just happening to have my shark repellent spray handy.

So, I chose to wear my underpants beneath my trousers
and although the world lost a potential super-hero
I found that I was liked and respected;
not needing to fight on top of skyscrapers
or defy death too many times to mention:
only needing to be me and to occasionally write poems
that go something like these.

Breakdown

She cried.
Rivers.
Constantly flowing like
Summer holiday traffic
until, like motorways,
everything came to a halt
and even though you'd cried
so much that your mascara
had been washed away
your eyes still looked up and said
"I love you"
as your salty fingers
gently touched my cheek
knowing that my shoulder was not
hard.

Figuratively Speaking

If I speak in pictures
then your ears must be my canvas
and my tongue a brush that paints the words
I want you to imagine.

Two Fingers

If you met Jesus what would you do?
Would you stick two fingers up at him
and tell him to go to hell?

Because if you would
he'd probably stick two fingers back up at you
and quietly say "I've already been"
except his 'V' would be for 'Victory'

Once Upon a Time Ago

Once
there was a time
when you could not let go
and neither could I.

But now
I have let go
and as I walk away
I find you scratching my back.

Teenage Dream

The speakers sing my favourite song
in earbashing stereo.

I stand before a mirror
tennis racquet firmly in hand
pretending to be something I am not
but something I would like to be.

Stalemate

I could not give you what you needed
because you could not give me what I needed.

I could not wipe away your tears
because you could not make me smile.

I could not erase your problems with a kiss
because your touch did not erase mine.
I could not help you bear your pressure
because my pressure was also great.

A look, the hint of a smile,
the yearning for a true loving touch
kept us silent and expecting
but as we expected
no unexpected surge of compassion surprised us
and we were left wanting, needing

I could not give you what you needed
because you could not give me what I needed.

I was on my high horse
but your castle was too far out of reach.

Remembrance

This year I had no poppy.
I don't know why
but I had nothing to put in my buttonhole
to remind me of the dying
so that I could live in freedom,
live like this today.
No red poppy to remind me
of the blood that was spilt.
No not even silence,
I didn't even stand to attention
for two minutes to ponder the bravery.

This year I had no poppy
but I do not need a red flower
to remind me that someone died
so that I might have life
and have it more abundantly.
My buttonhole may be empty
but my heart is full because everyday
I remember.

If Our Kisses Were Words

If our kisses were words
then we could write them down
and give them to each other
so that we could read them in times of loneliness
and feel the other's presence near.

However our kisses are kisses
and we can only reflect upon
the beauty of those moments shared.

Waiting for the Zap

I'm waiting for the ZAP!
to hit me full in the face and wake me up.
I'm waiting for thunderbolt to CRASH !
into my heart and jolt me into action.
I'm waiting for the morning when I awake with a BANG!
and I'm really on FIRE !
but my faith keeps going off phphut
and fiz z l i n g o u t

Where is He Now?

From an angel who liked light
he worked his way down
to a serpent that liked apples.
And down through the ages he progressed
through various stages of goathood
and guest appearance on the silver screen
until now
hardly anybody takes him seriously at all,
laughing at a horned gentleman
with a tail and three pronged fork
who wears red thermal underwear.
Which is just what he wants
as ouija boards are passed over the counter
in high street shops
and heavy metal priests
dramatise fire, brimstone, death and hell
from their records on display at Woolworths.

Jesus Knew

Jesus knew what he was talking about
when he said

"The first shall be the last and the last shall be first"

It's a pity that we don't know
what on earth he was talking about
because then we might not quote so readily that

"It's easier for a camel to pass through
the eye of a needle than it is
for a rich man to enter into the Kingdom of God."

Jesus Sat Reading Marx

Jesus sat reading Marx with a smile
and more than a feeling of familiarity.

Jesus pondered the idea of communism
remembering how well it had worked for the twelve and himself.

Jesus agreed with the notion of equal opportunity
and help for those who couldn't help themselves,
remembering his sermon on the mount.

Jesus sat and looked at twentieth century communism
and was filled with sadness.
The tears ran down his cheeks
as he saw how his ideas
had been mixed up, watered down
turned inside out and right around.
He saw how he had been rejected and discounted
and how the freedom to acknowledge him
had been withdrawn with vengeance and violence.

He saw the failure, the evil and the foolishness of man.
He saw the possibilities that were there
but saw the hate, the coldness and the selfishness
and he cried blood for those locked away.
He saw man's inhumanity to man
and he saw how his love was missing and ignored
and because of this he saw the failure.

And he was angry.
Gentle Jesus meek and mild was angry.
He saw what they had done to him
and what they had done to those who loved him
and gentle Jesus meek and mild was angry.
And gentle Jesus clenched his fist
and looked exactly the same as he did
on the day that he cleansed the temple.

A Personal Habit From Those Teenage Years That Will Not Go Away.

They told me I would grow out of it.
They told me it would be different later.
They told me I would change.
They told me it was just an adolescent phase
that I would pass through
and be embarassed about in years to come.

But they were wrong.
I didn't grow out of it.
I don't think differently
and even though I have changed
I'm not in the least bit embarassed
because even now, more than fifteen years on
- over 21 and still into Noddy -
I still think Slade bash out a rousing good tune.

Baby Baby Baby

There are meaningful sounding words
sung in meaningful sounding voices
over meaningful sounding music
that in trying too hard to be meaningful
means nothing at all to me.

And then there are words
that look meaningless and nonsensical
when written down but when put together with a melody
that sticks in the throat
that sticks in the throat
and spins around and round in the mind
and spins around and round in the mind
they can become magical
and altogether meaningful.

They might not change the world
but jaunty tunes to whistle
and happy rhymes to singalong
can get you through the day
and that's a start.

War Without Bloodshed

Peace, love and understanding
are words that roll easily off the tip of the tongue
into an acceptable idealistic cliche
that becomes bland with familiarity.

It is very easy to talk of peace and war
saying that war is definitely wrong
and that we long for peace,
until we realise that peace does not just mean
an absence of wars and guns and bloodshed
but a presence of love, caring, forgiveness
and a general coming to terms with the differences within us.

And if we do not have this presence
then all we will have is the war without the bloodshed
and the peace without the love and understanding
...which is not peace at all.

More Than a Badge

If all you know is a slogan
and you try to give it breath,
but you don't wear your heart on your sleeve
but a well pressed badge instead ...

If you're seen at all the right meetings
when you're strong with all the rest
but alone your hands are an open apology
instead of the militant fist ...

If you've got the right haircut and fashion,
the look to go with the views,
but then ignore what others say
because they don't look the same as you ...

If you've got the right papers and posters,
the records with the relevant words,
but all you do is read and tap your feet
when you're hoping to change the world ....

If it's style instead of life-style
your commitment part-time forget it.
It's got to be more than a badge and a book
if you're going to give your views credit.

Action speaks louder than words
and even if mine are barely heard
I'd rather be a glimmer of light or a spark
than hollow pose that's lost in the dark.
Yes, I'd rather be a glimmer that's straight from the heart
than a hollow pose that's lost in the dark.

Poem For The Militant Hypocrites

With furrowed brow and fervour
voices and hands held high
applauding those great principles
equality, democracy
and standing for the basic right
of freedom and free speech.

Yet when you're disagreed with
with words that are contentious
with views you term unbalanced
you stand up voices raised
in angry confrontation
and leave yourselves exposed.

You may as well go and drop your pants
bend down and turn your backs
because you know hypocrisy
has shown you to be talking through your ass.

The Need for Miracles is Now More Than Ever

With sharp swift slices, accurate and calculated,
the operation is complete.
No anaesthetic, no preparation
and no aftercare.
Open heart surgery is deemed successful
as the life giving organ
is efficiently replaced by a shiny clean
expensive metallic cash register.

And somewhere in the distance
a widow with two coins and a cancer condition
prays for the hem of a garment to touch.

The Lord Street Ruffle

The fur-ruffled cat stalks in green-ruffled grass
while hair-ruffled ladies with shop-ruffled bags
pass tear-ruffled children with mud-ruffled knees
on car-ruffled streets with breeze-ruffled trees.
Love-ruffled teenagers with kiss-ruffled mouths
have smiled-ruffled faces and hug-ruffled clothes.
It's a sun-ruffled day on a wind-ruffled street
and the rush-ruffled people are rushed off their feet
and the wash-ruffled jeans that hang on the line
are waving goodbye to the cloud-ruffled sky.

Thoughts on a Rainsoaked Beach in June

The majestic silence, a peaceful king.
I pray he'll dry your tears and calm the storm inside your heart.
Summer rain on a gently breathing wind,
the whisper of wet sand beneath the spiralling patterns of my feet.

A bleak and ragged coastline hewn with emotion.
Golden domes adorned by spikey green mohicans.
Broken bottles and jagged plastic scar the patterned sand,
scattered shells and driftwood are left like a thousand unfinished dreams.

The intricacy of crustacean forms hold fascination
for my wondering mind: lifeless eyes, brittle casing
unflexed pinchers, multi jointed appendages, no longer used
looking for all the world like an airfix model I made when I was young.

The lure of the gently lapping ocean.
The magic pull of the beckoning waves.
Memories of paddling barefoot with Wendy,
sharing ambitions and dreams that may be fulfilled one day.

Memories of picnics and crazy games of cricket
and splashing with the laughing smiling children
who for two weeks every Summer have the time of their lives
laughing and shrieking as Geoffrey gets buried in the sand.

Remembered laughter and magic moments,
momentarily lost in the echoes of a distant bell.
And the majesty of silence is enthralling,
and nothing is forgotten, remaining like holiday snapshots that I'm
flicking through on a rainsoaked beach in June...

Just Ask Alexander

When those who say belief God and Christianity
is just a crutch to lean on and help you easily
I'll say just ask Alexander.

When those who say the church is soft then maybe I'll agree
but don't tar all with that same brush because of what you've seen.
Just ask Alexander.

When those who say religion has caused injustice by its piety
I'll say yes but that is our abuse of what we are called to be.
Just ask Alexander.

If God is dead then what's the threat of a lifeless deity?
Why the need to rob their freedom if it's just a fallacy?
Just tell Alexander.

Tell that to a man inside a cell
who believes in heaven but lives in hell.
Tell that to the man whose body bears
savage beatings, bruises, scars.
Tell that to a man whose hunger strike
for a Bible was a fruitless fight.
Tell that to a man whose only crime
is sharing the love of one crucified.
But never ever ever tell him that it's easy.

More Than Just a Poem

The trouble with being a poet is
that I find when I meet someone special
who begins to hold sway in my thoughts,
romance inevitably leads to poetry
and my head is filled with rhyming couplets,
silken metaphors, intimate imagery
and the magic of moments spent idly holding hands.
Poems become frequent occasions on the lovers' calendar,
causing late nights in search of the right expression
that describes the moment perfectly
and conveys the peace and beauty of our friendship.

And when the time arrives and we must tread our separate paths,
again the poems besiege me
like the constant knocking on a door that wishes to stay locked.
Expressions of depression are wrenched and pulled
from the very depths of my heart.
Metaphors of sadness, like bad teeth,
are painfully extracted, roots and all,
without the anaesthetic to reveal
a numbed and aching soul stripped bare,
a nerve exposed for all to see,
prodded by the poet's pen, each slow deliberate stroke prolonged
drawing out the pain and punishing each sentence,
to leave an open, hollow void
that love once filled with sweetness but now has left decayed.
Meanwhile, the passion and the pain is chipped away and sculpted,
chiselled by the wordsmith into art to be admired,
and memories and feelings become public
and the secrecy of love once shared is savage.

So you see, that's the trouble with being a poet.
Special friends and lovers
and those with whom I've shared a bond
may find themselves as characters
or subjects for my similes,
as public memories or reasons for my loneliness,
as boy meets girl meets poem
and romance blossoms not into a long and meaningful loving
relationship but a long and meaningful, loving poem,
blooming like a phoenix from the ashes.

And that is why I do not really want
to write a poem for you,
although I fear I have,
because you are more than just a poem for this poet,
more than just a shared experience translated into pretty words,
and our love is more than metaphors,
more than just a poem for this poet
much, much more.

Palm Leaves

You laid palm leaves before me
welcoming my every move
but they only served to soften the blow
of your execution of my love.

And not for the first time
the love that was supposed to lie down and die
did not.

Every Name Under the Sun

You can call me every name under the sun
and insult me until your tongue is dry of derivatives.
You can swear at me until you are blue in the face.
You can hit me until I am blue in the face
but you will not offend me half as much
as when you say the words
"God" or "Jesus Christ"
without even a hint of love in your voice.

1989 - 1990

Poems From a Lover's Diary

Poems From a Lover's Diary

Even in my wildest dreams I couldn't conceive
of anything better than this.
Nightingales sing and church bells ring when we hold hands,
planets collide and symphonies crash when we kiss.
When I'm with you my heart loops the loop
there's a bright sun shining high and the sky is always blue.

When we can see the everyday becomes special
and the mundane becomes exciting:
When kisses still thrill after the thousandth
and hands still itch to be held.
When watching T.V. with a cup of tea
is as natural and easy as breathing
then maybe, just maybe, we'll have something close to love.

And like the familiarity of a favourite mug,
the sound of a classic single from 1973
the comfort of a well worn T shirt
and the cosiness of my continental quilt
you could say that I'm beginning to feel at home with you
my love.

You smile at my greatest obsession
listening to "Cum on feel the noize"
While Batman and Robin escape a sticky end once more.
Close by Frank and little frank
are joining forces with Lord Emsworth and the Empress of Blandings
in an attempt to regain my attention
while I smile at you, my greatest obsession.

If there is no greater feeling in the world
than being loved and being in love
then in that moment when a kiss becomes total abandonment
heaven is glimpsed for a split split second.

You haven't even gone yet
and my lips feel dry already,
as if they haven't been kissed in weeks.
I don't think I'll get used to making tea for one
and suddenly the sofa's a very big and lonely place to be.
Still, I'll lick my lips in anticipation,
put a teabag in your favourite mug
and try to warm the sofa
as I count the days, the hours, the seconds
until you come back home to me.

> Florida, Harrogate,
> What's the difference anyway?
> What's a few thousand miles between friends?
> Not half as much as a few thousand miles between lovers.
> You in Florida
> me in Harrogate.
> Neither of us at home
> and neither of us feeling completely at home where we are.

Even the cricket became interesting.
Knowing that I haven't got to tidy the front room
or make the tea before you arrived
lulled me into welcome lethargy.
I'll just watch this next over I lied to myself
as I thought of things that didn't really need doing
until just before you got back.

> As fast as the speed of sound
> Your words sped across the ocean and into my room.
> And in those moments thousands of miles meant nothing.
> Sixteen days meant nothing
> and the hours writing poetry about you meant nothing
> as everything faded into the background of your words.

I have rehearsed that moment a thousand times.
That moment when we forget sixteen days apart.
That moment when our eyes meet.
That moment when our arms reach out.
That moment when time will stand still.
That moment when tears mingle, cheeks rub and lips kiss.
That moment will be ours.
I have rehearsed that moment a thousand times
and will rehearse it a thousand times more
before it finally arrives.

I might as well be missing an arm or something.
It's just that part of me feels elsewhere at the moment,
far far away, everyday
and quiet moment when thoughts drift uninterrupted
bangs that nail home once more.

I want to look in your eyes once more,
look deeply and see that they are the same as they were.
I want to look into your eyes once more
just to make sure that they're the same as I remember them.
And when I have done that I will smile widely,
close my eyes and kiss you till I can breathe no more.

Mush mush mush mush.
That's all I've written lately.
Soppy mushy stuff about you not being here.
I'll be glad when you get home
and I can start to write about more cheerful things again.

Apprehension and love walk hand in hand
and like any other step of faith
our hearts pound faster
with the excitement and knowledge
of making the right move.

The lips that melted yours
That mouth that breathed upon your neck.
The tongue that sent shivers down your spine

faltered

and for once was nervous,
shyness bubbling up from deep within.

And still my heart beat faster.
Still my lips tremble
and my mind dashes like a fly around a light.
Still I swallow hard and blink my eyes in disbelief
trying to drink it all in.

And yet I know that this is right
and am still.

I am torn between running to the nearest rooftop
and shouting loud for all to hear
or retreating to a quiet room
with a pen, some thoughts and a smile.

Either way, it makes no difference
I'm just in love with you
and the ring upon your finger
chimes that news for everyone to see.

1990

Storming the Archives

1990 and You

1990 sounds frightening.
A new year.
A new decade.
A new bunch of ideals and resolutions
that I'll never live up to.

1990 sounds exciting.
The year we marry.
The year we begin.
The year we'll never regret
no matter what happens.

1990 sounds great.
Frightening.
Exciting.
And you.

Batman Never Comes to Retford

Batman never comes to Retford
not because there is no crime
but with all the trouble in Gotham.
He hasn't got the time.

Robin never comes to Retford
not because there is no crime
but with all the trouble in Gotham
he's always helping Batman.

Spiderman never comes to Retford
not because there is no crime
but being used to New York City there's no tall buildings
in Retford to attach his webs to.

Rebel Fifties Giant Poem

I'm the James Dean of the poetry world
not one of those crashing bores
but I die very early at every gig
a rebel without applause.

A Trival Pursuit

I cried when my father took a fold out poster
disgusted that I'd paid the princely sum
of fifteen new decimal pence for it
and used it as a doormat in my own bedroom.
His slippered feet trampled on the smiling grins of heroes,
Dave, Don, Jimmy and Noddy.
Silver suits and mirrored hats seemed to lose their sparkle
as he feet went back and forth, his head shaking with disbelief.

My mother rescued the poster
and although it never smiled down
from my bedroom wall at home
I kept it safe and precious and when the time was right
put it up with relish and with pride
revelling in the knowledge that trivia is really truly worthless
and really truly wonderful at that.

Thanks for the Memory

I can remember that moment now.
Exactly where I was when I found out
that Slade were straight in at number one.
Tarleton High School form room, Tuesday lunchtime,
a crowd gathered expectantly around a crackling transistor.
Listening ears hungry for the latest sounds.
It was always the same,
play the top four records in reverse order
then the top forty countdown before the number one.
As soon as we heard that 10CC's "Rubber Bullets"
was down at two we knew.
Riproaring opening chords widened smiles and lit a fuse
that sent us reeling and rocking
like lighted jumping jacks around school furniture.
Pretend electric guitars, imaginary drums
but living a raucous chorus
as we joined the lads we loved so well:
"You know how to skweeze me woah oh...
You know how to pleeze me woah oh..."

And in those moments we lost ourselves,
tiny heads full to the brim of jangling ripchord melody
torn from lungs made of leather and given life
by a voice that sounded like razorblades and gravel in a cementmixer.
Unbroken voices strained as one, word perfect and utterly joyful.

The funny thing is
I can only remember one person in that room,
Ian Hornby, nicknamed Zombus for some reason.
The rest, their names and faces have faded with the onset of years
but I know that in those chorus moments
something special lingered
and even now, over a decade later,
my spine still tingles as those opening chords
light again the fuse
that makes pop snap crackle rock and roll once more.

The Twenty Third of September Nineteen Eighty Nine

With a best man who looked like
he'd hired his shirt from Big Daddy
and his waistcoat from Ronnie Corbett
you waited to say your vows.

Looking her full in the face
as he did with you
promises were boldly spoken
and proudly repeated for all to hear.

Kneeling for prayers
brought a blessing of mirth from friends
unable to ignore your shoes
H E on one, L P on the other.

As you said
not one to overstate the obvious
you forgot to say how beautiful your bride looked
but we knew that anyway.

Those crazy wild smiles
dancing to "Merry Christmas Everybody"
on the 23rd September 1989
will not easily be forgotten

and as you walked out together
to face the future as one
I couldn't help but hold my lover close
look forward to that day when we will do the same
and pray that we too may have the warmth
of special friends who know the love we've found.

The Happiest Days of My Life

When Ron Ely was the best Tarzan ever
and Pete Duel was still alive and well as Hannibal Hayes.
When Summers had fifteen hours of golden sunshine every day
and Winters were crispy with drifting snow.
When football was played at all times in all seasons
and Slade were forever top of the charts.
When innocence was laughing at the word bum
and believing that a kiss could make a baby.

Those were the days.

When hide and seek wasn't cissy,
bike rides were fighter squadrons,
home made go karts and bow and arrows
were the just the best things in the world,
when my dad built goal post with nets
and marked out a pitch in our back garden.

Those were the days my friends, happy days.
"The happiest days of your life," someone said
"Remember them well."

But these are the happiest days of my life.
Days filled with forgiveness and newness of spirit,
the knowledge and touch of a woman so special
I'm not even going to try and describe her.
The understanding and strength of family
and the joy of new lives within it,
still buying all Slades records
and still playing football in all seasons.

Yes, these are the happiest days of my life
and I hope and pray
that each time I look longingly over my shoulder on old times,
good old heartwarming priceless times,
that I will be able to turn back
and look you full in the face and say
"Yes, those days were truly great
but these are the happiest days of my life."

The Weekend my House Became an Adventure Playground

The house may be tidy.
The ornaments may be safe.
The ghost from up the chimney is gone
letter box monster no longer frightens
and my neighbours are probably
glad of the peace and quiet.
The patter of tiny feet,
neice and nephew's to be precise,
sounded more like a herd of angry elephants
in steel rimmed clogs
ridden by hyenas high on laughing gas.
Before breakfast.

Yes, the house may be tidy.
The ornaments may be safe
but those little sparks of infant joy
that energised this room
into a battlezone for Ghostbusters
and a car chase for the Batmobile
have taken home with them
a tiny piece of happiness from us all
but trodden oven chips into my carpet.

Hide and seek with dirty linen baskets
blazing smiles from a fireman's helmet,
puddled slides and a mini marathon
running in new wellington boots.
A rainy funfair day, all rides and cuddly toys
and a little girl with sticky hands in mine
who asked if she could have more cloud to eat.
"Look I've got a brew" she proudly said
pointing to a mark upon her leg.
"Don't you mean a bruise?" asked Daddy
"No I've only got one."

Yes indeed, the house may be tidy.
The ornaments may be safe
and we may be safe
and we may well be able
to visit the bathroom uninterrupted.
The oven chips may be swept up
and breakfast may be civilised.
Silence may be golden
but the laughter of children is priceless.

When ....

When tender moments do not coincide
and the right thing is said
but at the wrong time and in the wrong tone of voice.

When emotions go unnoticed
and efforts are overshadowed
by more immediate concerns.

When a touch doesn't touch
but interrupts
awkwardly.

When conversations drift aimlessly
all niceties and humdrum
and words are trip-wires.

When it is clear that although our mouths are open
although our fingers touch
nothing is said or done
and we do not communicate.

When this happens
all I want to do is hold you
gently hold you for as long as it takes
until our minds are free
and we can speak and kiss again.
With feeling.

The First Time We Make Love.

The first time we make love
I want to laugh like there's no tomorrow,
thrill with the excitement of the big dipper,
roller coaster and ghost train all rolled into one.
Roar like a lion singing Slade's greatest hits.
Feel the love of God in every tightened muscle.
Taste the taste of heaven with each kiss.
Burn more brightly than a forest fire,
have all the grace and splendour of shooting star at night
and return to earth like a falling feather.
The first time we make love I want us to sweat.
Buckets.

The first time we make love
I want us to cry the tears of joy
when we become one being
and the first time we make love
it will be, it must be
and I know with all my heart
that it shall be forever.

Trust, Love and Sex Sneak Preview the Afterlife

I have tasted Heaven.
When our bodies rise and fall in perfect unison
and rhythm and control is not our own.
When abandonment is total and passion is trust.
When chemicals react and nature sparks,
new colours clash and dazzle
senses raw and vivid, drink each second in
struggling for breath in awesome ecstasy
yet savouring the flavours sweet and new.

In all this
and the even more that words cannot convey
I have tasted heaven
we have tasted heaven
peaked at the Promised Land
reeled in the face of beauty
we have tasted heaven
sipping briefly on new wine.

And one day sometime soon
when in the kingdom presence
each second will be this pure
and eternity too short
to drink each second fully.

No Amount of Poetry Substitutes Your Presence

If you were here with me now
I would surely kiss you goodnight.

If you were here with me now
I would surely tell you how much I love you.

If you were here with me now
I would surely hold you tight.

If you were here with me now
this poem would surely be a blank piece of paper
emotionless and empty.

No amount of poetry substitutes your presence.

Archaeology For Lovers

Unearthing dead bare memories
excavating long gone corpses
sharing secret skeletons
from so deep inside
it almost fractures to reveal.

And as our strength and love
are made from blood and life
these ghosts will never haunt
there is and never will be
resurrection for these bones.

Skeletons removed carefully from closets
are laid to rest eternally
in deep fathomless graves
the dirt trampled down and forgotten
and immortality is ours to keep unscathed

Drunk On The Wine of Friendship

Empty glasses
and the fullness of friendship
laughter like the peal of wedding bells
and spirits full of warmth.

Empty glasses
happiness swimming
like infants in the rivers
on hot Summer's days
not wanting to get out.

Empty glasses
special bonds and feelings
smiles embrace the hearts
without the violins.

Empty glasses
no sunsets to walk off to
no sentimental roses
no soppy emotion
just a room full of friends

The Timing on God's Watch is Always Perfect

When the time is right
everything will fall neatly into place,
barriers will simple fade away
and the cogs will gently slip together
gliding into peaceful action.

When the time is right
understanding will be perfect if not complete,
assurance will feel like the sunshine
and joy will sing like creation
on that resurrection morning.

When the time is right
love will enter like fire
and fly like an eagle
cleansing the depths
and soaring to the highest peaks.

When the time is right
old things will pass away unnoticed
the past will be unmissed
the future be unmissable
and the present unbelievable.

When the time is right
spirits will be filled
with peace and power celestial
the newness be eternal
and faith will be unshakeable.

And when this time has come
grasp it with both hands and mind
and hold it in your heart
for only you will truly know
for only you can truly wait
for only then are you truly ready
when the time is really truly right.

And the Lord God Moved to Brentwood

On the seventh day God rested and saw that it was good.
Quite a long time after the seventh day God looked again and wasn't so sure. It wasn't as good as he thought. Perhaps Bethlehem wasn't the ideal birthplace for his son and maybe the Jews weren't the chosen people after all

And lo the Lord God Almighty began to doubt his judgement and saw that he needed a change. And Lo the Lord God Almighty packed his bags, uprooted the pearly gates and built a new Jerusalem. In Brentwood, Essex. Closing his eyes tightly he put his index finger on a map of England and Lo another special people were chosen. From Ormskirk, a small market town in Lancashire. Churches closed, houses were sold as pilgrims flocked to the new promised land.

After setting up a new and better church the Lord God Almighty decided that he'd get a job in the City that paid well enough for him to have large barbecue parties on his large patio with his chosen people. He bought his son a filofax, a personal computer and a brand new top of the range Volvo with quadrophonic digital stereo, electric push button windows and built in car telephone.

Together they joined the golf club and played off a handicap of seven although with extensive practising for forty days and forty nights did this eventually become three then one. At this point God began to doubt his omnipresence, only being able to take one shot at a time, whereas before he could have played a sand wedge on the thirteenth while putting for a birdie on the second at the same time watching Jack Nicklaus sink the winning shoot in the American Open. Now it took him all his time to get a par on the seventh. There had once been victory at the eighteenth green hill far away in three but that was lost in the mists of time.

And setting the video the Lord God Almighty put his feet up and saw that it was good. Very good indeed, as he put the finishing touches to the guest list for the weekend party. Checking the trifle and the gateaux he saw that they were good as well. A touch more cream and lo they were even better.

Taking his headphones he listen to a tape of a recent service and smiled. It was good to hear the heavenly singing and tearful prayers. He just wished you could get four hour cassettes.
Pressing the remote control the video came to life. The film was old and grey, lined and worn, filmed in black and white. Time to tape over this one thought the Lord God Almighty as he fast forwarded from something called "The Sermon on the Mount."

Before dropping off to sleep he remembered how he used to get out more. Ethiopia, South Africa, Calcutta, London Bridge in the early hours. He hadn't even visited the hospital recently but then again life was very busy in Brentwood, what with four three hour services a week plus work and barbecues. And Brentwood was his chosen place.

On his days off the Lord God Almighty began to rewrite the Bible on computer and wipe clean all his old home movie videos. And behold he saw that it was comfortable, very comfortable indeed thank you very much.

Dave Hill Never Played Football, Alan Ball Never Played Lead Guitar

Football doesn't mix with fashion.
At least it didn't in the seventies.
Participants in playgrounds games may looked good
from a distance
but to all intents and purposes the skill factor and been sacrificed.

Platform shoes did not enhance ball control
positively discouraging the delicate touches
of a teenage Duncan Mackenzie,
George Best style dribbling
or a Bobby Charlton powerblaster volley.
Direction was impossible to forecast accurately
regarding six inch platform zip up boots
although they did help with high crosses and crunching challenges.
Mind you five minutes running round in them
and you were well knackered.

It wasn't just the shoes.
Flared trousers against the wind became more like hang gliding.
Even on still days it was difficult to find your shoes underneath them.
And there was always the danger that the football could get lost
up a particular wide pair, sometimes for a whole dinnertime.
Having to take three steps before the trousers moved
didn't assist long driving runs beating round three players and the goalie
but could on occasions fool the opposition's offside trap.

Football and fashion doesn't mix.
Yesterday, today or forever.
The moral of the story ... simple :

If you want to be good at playground football at school
forget about fashion, shop at Marks and Spencers.
Plus the school photographs won't be as embarrassing
to look back on in twenty years time.

I Want to Write Poetry Like Peter Reid Plays Football

I want to write poetry
like Peter Reid plays football
never flinching from a challenge
or afraid to tackle head on.
Always giving one hundred per cent.

I want to write poetry
like Peter Reid plays football
never giving in, never overawed
and never afraid of mixing it with the best.
and be an inspiration to those around me.

I want to attack with skill
break down your defences
be proud of my colours
I want to have the heart of a lion
the wisdom of an experienced campaigner
and the guts of never say die fighter.
Hard as nails but always fair
I want to write words that win hearts
words that delight and thrill
words that hit the target
and words worth looking at again.

I want to write poetry
like Peter Reid plays football
but I never ever ever
want to resort to wearing Grecian 2000.

Star Trek Fifteen : The Search for Senility.

Captain's log stardate 38 ... and a bit. These are the voyages of the Starship Enterprise : to boldly go where no one has gone before and discover strange new worlds and civilisations ... all of whom speak American English, breathe clear oxygen and live on planets made from papier-mache and sand.

Captain James T Kirk, veteran commander has just had his hair permed again, but is looking worried. He paces up and down stroking his chin as he ponders the problem, possibly one of the greatest dilemnas the Captain has ever faced. Horrors of horrors, not only does the planet they've discovered not have American English as their native tongue and breathe oxygen, but the same set was used the previous week to fend off the advances of green men with high foreheads and silver cloaks who were exploiting the hairy Neanderthals. But these problems are minuscule compared to the one in hand. Far far worse than any of these this planet has no attractive female aliens for the debonair Captain to fall in love with and nearly forsake the Enterprise for.

There were, however, several six tentacled one eyed scaly brown lizard tailed creatures who projectile vomited whenever they opened their mouths but he couldn't be sure they were female.

Having decided this, the landing party about to beam down was cancelled which was a great relief to the nameless crewman who had joined the Captain, Bones and Spock. The nameless crewman breathed a sigh of relief as he knew only too well that the only time a new crew member was allowed on the landing party was when hostile alien forces would be hiding ready to ambush and take life. And it was never the Captain, Bones or Spock who got killed.

Spock meanwhile raising one eyebrow thoughtfully affirms that it is indeed affirmative and logically appropriate to discontinue the present exploratory probe until such time when a positive affirmative can be administered with absolute confidence, ultimate precision and necessary consideration for the innate right of life to persist in universal harmony on a galactic scale.

McCoy says he wishes Spock would talk in English.

Just then lights flash at Uhuru's desk and the broad tones of Scottie rang out clearly: "I cannae hold her any longer Cap'n, we're losing power, I think she's gonna blow."

Captain James T. Kirk remains calm as only captains can in crises like these as he seeks out answers to the problems of the Universe:

Can the Starship Enterprise possibly be aerodynamic?

What have crimpelene V neck Manchester City football shirts, short skirts, black tights and knee length high heeled leather boots to do with space travel?

Do the clangers really exist?

Is there a legal retirement age for crew members or does it depend on the number of films and videos sold?

Measles Don't Come Giftwrapped

As a child I was never ill on schooldays.
It was always holidays.
Always.
I remember one Christmas morning
leaping from my bed to find
what good old Father Christmas had given me
only to find he'd given me
a battery operated racing car on a lead
so that it would travel three feet
at one mile an hour
then do a back somersault.
I'd drive it cross country
thanks to knees, pillows and bed clothes
and I drove it cross country
thanks to knees, pillows and bed clothes
all Christmas because good old Father Christmas
had also given me measles.
Why me ?
And why hadn't my brothers and sisters got them ?
Or mum and dad ?
What had I done ?
And I began to wonder if Father Christmas
really did get to know
about all the naughty things that children did
and if so
how on earth did he find out
about that shaky thing with snow in
that I had dropped and broken
on the living room carpet
then blamed it on my sister
who then got smacked and sent to bed.

Back at school
teacher asked us about Christmas.
I told her Father Christmas had given me
a battery operated racing car and measles.
One boy said that he'd been sick all Christmas
and that he couldn't stop going to the toilet for five days
and I wondered what he'd done wrong.

All Mothers Have Long White Beards and Bright Red Duffle Coats

Christmas Day
always began early in our house.
Sometimes very very early
when it was still Dark Time
First we would look to the foot of the bed
Where a sock would be full and bulging
(Strangely enough this was the only time
of the year when we would request
one of dad's size ten wellington boot socks)
The sock would contain breakfast :
tangerines, nuts, a small chocolate bar and more tangerines
plus several other small items like
a pack of cards, a biro or a torch.
We would practise morse code messages with the torch
and mum and dad would always interpret them as meaning
Christmas day did not officially begin until half past seven.
After what seemed like decades
We would be allowed into the living room
where we could find our very own
personalised sacks from Santa himself
with our very own personal messages from Santa himself:
"To Paul, Happy Christmas from Santa"
although I must admit I was somewhat confused
and was convinced that Father Christmas
was actually a woman because the message
was always written in my mum's best handwriting.

It is only now that I realise
that my theory is not as stupid
or as far fetched as it sounds
and that it is indeed mothers
who work the hardest over Christmas.

I Used to Watch With Mother

I used to watch with mother
and she could never answer all my questions
like how Hammy Hamster and Roddy Rat
could sail boats, drive cars and speak in English.
Or why the Woodentops were always woodentopless
and just what made the biggest Spotty Dog you ever did see
move in that most original manner.
It amazed me that Windy Miller was never garotted
and that the Trumpton Fire Brigade
(Pugh Pugh Barney McGrew Cuthbert Dibble Grub)
never actually put a fire out
but spent most of their time rescuing cats
or removing branches from Chippy Minton's roof.
You'd never see Mister Benn in his underwear
and where did that shopkeeper come from?
And why was it that whenever I was off school
it was always the episode where he became a pirate.
Either that or The Herbs when Pashana Bedhi
lost his snake and Baileaf
(I'm the gardener I work from early morn
  you'll find me sweeping up the leaves
  or tidying the lawn)
mistook it for a hosepipe.
I always thought Bill and Ben
should have subtitles.
The only word I ever recognised was
Slobadodge ... Slowcoach the tortoise
and which one had the high voice ?
Can you remember children ?
was it Bill? Or was it Ben?
Or was it the talking plant that could only say "Weeeeed"?
Which brings us on to Pogle's Wood.
How come the plant could not only talk
but how did it decide that
"Plant like bilberry wine "?
Had it ever tasted lager ?
No wonder it preferred bilberry wine.

And if Pippin was a boy what was Tog?
My favourite was always Camberwick Green
"Here is a box, a musical box,
wound up and ready to play ..."
I used to love guessing who would be inside.
I wanted to grow up like Captain Snort of Pippin Fort
as I liked the red uniform and blonde pigtails
and the fact that a drum sounded
every time you took a step.
Plus I wanted to be "Driving along in my army truck,
a humperty bumperty army truck ... "

I used to watch with mother
and still do occasionally
remembering magic words like "Herbidacious"
and singing along with Dill the dog
and a very friendly lion called Parsley.
I guess I'm just a great big sentimental old Hector.

All Memories Are Boxed Away for Rainy Days

Looking through dusty boxes in my parent's attic
I found keys that ground inside those rusty locks
creaking open once forgotten doors.
Almost familiar rooms with sketchy recollections
that all of us possess blinking in the daylight
and coughing, breathing in fresh air.

I found books from twenty years ago,
The Hotspur Book for Boys, Lancashire Soccer
and a host of Tarzan, Popeye, Rupert and Blue Peter Annuals.

Unfolding Popswop pages
I saw Slade as they should always be remembered,
resplendent and gaudy, glittering in all their
stack heeled yobbish glory.

Primary School topic books,
The History of Aviation in eleven chapters,
thirty two pages and several newspaper cuttings
and Famous Battles from the Trojan War
to World War Two in twenty three short pages
and a number of very large illustrations.

Notepads full of early poems screaming to be read
bulging with naivete, heartfelt love and yearning,
idealism a proud and bold market square evangelist
shouting loud and blinkered
communicating little.

All of these were keys to the same lock
that pushed that door much wider
shading in the colours
as storylines and passages, poems and occasions
shifted into focus with clarity perfected.
Old friends were rediscovered.
Old stories were relived
Old heroes reawakened
as childhood was revived.

Looking through these dusty boxes
I realised that none of this
had really been forgotten
but filed and boxed away in an attic marked 'Memories'
and stored especially for a rainy day
such as this one.

School Reunion

Fourteen years is a long time when you've been away.
Since I left secondary school and with it a group of friends
some of whom shared early primary years as well.
In the name of further education and employment
I pulled up my roots and moved away
to eventually buy a house and marry
just like many of those I'd left behind.

Fourteen years is a long time and then to walk into that room
and recognise those smiles on faces framed with more weight or less hair
time melted and it could have been last week
as familiar jokes and stories flowed
nicknames remembered while real names lurked on the tips of tongues
the old days were dragged up laughing
and the in between days penciled to the present.

Fourteen years is a long time and some of those friendships
go back even further, the best part of a quarter of a century
and even though we never kept in touch one thing is for sure
nothing is ever truly lost or totally forgotten.
The passing of time may blur the recollection
but one nickname, one joke, one story
is all that it takes to pull that trigger
to bring it all back home as memories fly like bullets.

Fourteen years is a long time and I must admit the fact
that I was almost scared to face that room alone
in case you all had changed too much
in case I had changed too much
in case we had all changed too much
and in so doing would have nothing more to share
than dusty meaningless anecdotes and polite embarrassment.
It is one thing to share the past
and another to claim the present
so that our history is remembered and given relevance today
and if there is but one thing to learn it is this :
I am sure that it will not be fourteen years
before some of us meet again for longer.

Your Silence is Always Longer

I wish I had the strength
to ignore you for longer
but I always find myself
wanting to say "Sorry" first
even when it is not my fault.
You really can be a pain in the neck
and at times unreasonable,
refusing to talk or enter into any discussion.
Your silences are always longer
and more   awkward.
Just once I'd like to stay sullen
sulky
silent
for as long as it takes, probably days,
to be able to prove that point to you
but I'm far too soft
and I wish I had the strength
to ignore you for longer.
Sometimes.

The Clock That Watches Over Us is Feeding On Our Time and Growing Fat

The mundanities of life have eaten up our time to love.
The clock seems to have grown faster with the pace we live our lives
and the task we give ourselves seem to take forever.

There is still confetti in my car
trodden in by many months of dirt
bruised and torn from the everyday
faded, old and worn by the heaviness of use.
Occasionally when tidying deep beneath the seats
I'll find one piece untarnished
still looking fresh and white
a celebration article of love.

And it is these I search for now these days.
Moments as fresh as wedding day vows
where we are both fully alive to each other
and not exhausted from the strain of merely getting by.
Moments where our double bed
becomes a land that time forgets
full of fairy tale adventures instead of which
you are Sleeping Beauty and I am Rip Van Winkle.

Even as I write I can hear your troubled breathing
and sleep is not a sheet that can draw a discreet veil
across those touchy nerves we sometimes leave exposed.

Where once we used to burn so bright
our eyes were nearly blinded
now we spark from time to time
keeping to the rhythm of the ever ticking clock.

It's not that we have grown apart or love each other less
but more that we have unwittingly and readily accepted
the futile and the ordinary as normal
filling time like cramming extra boxes to the brim
with trinkets we do not wish to throw away
assuming that one day they all will find a use.

I love you more than I know and more than I show
yet still desire to love you more then ever
and if from time to time
we can throw that clock away
or at the very least cover it with blankets
then we will give ourselves the chance
to keep our home fires burning
and ready to blaze at any given moment
inextinguishable love that will burn the pointing fingers
scorch accusing hours
and savour the infinity we choose to spend within each other's arms.

Unknown Quantity

I don't think I will ever know
how much I really love you.

I have heard it said that
you only really appreciate someone when they're gone.

That would mean you would have to go
for me to appreciate you fully.

I do not want you to go.
At all.

So, I suppose I will never know
how much I really love you.

Suffice it to say that
I love you too much to let you go.

To Despise Yourself is Selfish, To Love Yourself is not

At those times when you are most unhappy with yourself
detesting the spots or the extra pound or two.
At those times when you screw your face up
while looking at your profile in the mirror and complain.
At those times when you scowl and resolve
to give up chocolate, putting yourself down.

It is these times when you dislike yourself
that you start to build a wall between us.
When you are not happy with yourself you are never happy
to accept that I can possibly be happy with you.
When you don't love yourself
then stop me from doing so fully.

It is true that one can only accept the love of another
if they have first accepted that they themselves are lovable
and it is also true that you will not believe that I believe in you
until you first have the self belief that allows it.
Thus it is we strive for that acceptance,
that pinnacle where doubt is banished out of sight.

The problem is that many of us are permanently struck partway
cradling our thoughts, accepting mediocrity
and blowing up inadequacies out of all proportion.
Enlarging the negatives and reducing the positives
so that all is out of focus and the colour drained away.

At those times when you look into that mirror
dissatisfied and down then just remember this:
that only when you accept the person you see before you
will you be ready to accept the love of someone else
and experience the specialness of being loved
that overlooks these blemishes anyway.

Understanding God a Bit

Understanding God a bit
is like listening to your all time favourite record
again and again and again.
You can listen to it a thousand times or more
and still hear something fresh
that you haven't quite heard in the same away before.
You can sing the words over and over
and still they take on new meanings.
You can remember the buzz
from the very first time you heard it
and the memories that return
Once you only knew the chorus
but now you not only know the verses word for word
but are getting to grips with the lead guitar break too.

Where once you didn't know why you liked it,
just that you did,
now you know that it is part of you,
the past, the present and the future
and that each time you hear it
your heart will miss a beat
goosebumps rise upon your arms
and shivers race down your spine
as body, soul and mind connect
for those few perfect minutes.

And so it is that listening to your favourite record
is like understanding God a bit more
each time you play it.

A Glimpse Of Heaven On a Yorkshire Landscape

The clouds parted
like a tear in the thick grey woollen blanket
that wrapped around our small forgotten corner of the world
and a solid shaft of light broke through
connecting earth and sky
that made the green greener
the colours sharper and the air clearer
and just for a moment
it looked for all the world as though
Jesus Christ Himself
was beaming down from heaven
just like Captain Kirk from the Starship Enterprise.

And in a way He was.

If I Could Have My Way

If I could have my way
this poem would have loud guitars
and an instant singalong chorus
that would become anthemic on the terraces.
It would be released
as a seven inch single only
with a equally good B side and no extended remix.

If I could have my way
this poem would reach number one
in its first week of release
and stay there for quite some time.
It would also reach into your home
give you a melody to sing
and thoughts you may consider.

If I could have my way
this poem would have Noddy Holder
singing The Gospel of Saint John
to the tune of "Merry Christmas Everybody"
And somewhere in the background
Jesus would plug in his guitar
tap his feet, smile and wait
for everyone to sing the words of his chorus.

Look to the future now
it's only just begun...

Find Yourself a Rainbow

I have started to touch my dreams.
Rainbows once to distant
no end and no beginning
unfinished out of focus
seem now full and almost
well within my grasp.

I have started to touch my dreams.
Ambitions from my youth
unreal and far away
needing my head up in the clouds
now live and breathe and take their shape
my feet down in the crowds.

This journey has been fifteen years or more.
What then seemed so impossible
is now those few small steps away
as dreams soft focus into hard reality
like precious snapshots gazed at every day

Yes I have started to touch my dreams
and in those waking moments
senses tingle goosebumps rise
as wiping sleep from tired tearful eyes
I stand beneath that rainbow
arms outstretched arms outstretched
my arms outstretched to heaven
knowing that it's very nearly time
knowing that the dream is almost mine
almost almost to scared to claim it
in case that rainbow turns to dust
or should that pot of gold be rust
but knowing that the dream is mine
I know I will I know I must
take that dream and name it
take that dream and name it
take that dream and name it
mine.

Poetry with a punch

Paul has performed extensively at schools, festivals, libraries, cabaret venues, pubs, arts centres, churches, radio stations and selected front rooms.

He is available for performances at schools, workshops, arts festivals, cabaret gigs, readings, national T.V. and radio and the opening of garden fetes and supermarkets.

MORE VERSATILE THAN BATMANS UTILITY BELT.

For more information write to:

Paul Cookson, 18 Hind Street, Retford, Notts. DN22 7EN
Tel: 0777 700248

BOOKS BY PAUL COOKSON

" Funny, direct and has a conscience. This poetry demands a response. "

STRAIT MAGAZINE

Sketches	Short poems with a personal touch. Price £1.50 (incl. p&p)
Batman and Oddy Available from 1st April	2nd edition of poems and short stories entering the world of Oddy at desk high level. 18 new pieces. Artwork by Cliff Woodcock Introduction by Mike Harding Price £3.85 (incl. p&p)
The Amazing Captain Concorde	Illustrated collection of poetry for children. Price £3.95 (incl. p&p)
Over 21 and Still into Noddy Available from 1st April	Selected poems 1979 - 1990 Introduction by Noddy Holder Price £5.30 (incl. p&p)

Available from
A TWIST IN THE TALE, 18 Hind Street, Retford, Notts. DN22 7EN
Tel: 0777 700248

Please make all cheques and postal orders payable to:-
'A Twist in the Tale."